Bhanu Prakash Lohani, Pradeep K. Kushwaha, Abhijeet Ashri, Mohit Aggarwal, Akhil V. Raj

Performance Study of Logically-Modified Heap Sort Algorithm

GRIN Publishing

Bibliographic information published by the German National Library:

The German National Library lists this publication in the National Bibliography; detailed bibliographic data are available on the Internet at http://dnb.dnb.de .

Imprint:

Copyright © 2014 GRIN Verlag GmbH
Print and binding: Books on Demand GmbH, Norderstedt Germany
ISBN: 978-3-656-84648-2

This book at GRIN:

http://www.grin.com/en/e-book/284417/performance-study-of-logically-modified-heap-sort-algorithm

GRIN - Your knowledge has value

Since its foundation in 1998, GRIN has specialized in publishing academic texts by students, college teachers and other academics as e-book and printed book. The website www.grin.com is an ideal platform for presenting term papers, final papers, scientific essays, dissertations and specialist books.

Visit us on the internet:

http://www.grin.com/

http://www.facebook.com/grincom

http://www.twitter.com/grin_com

Performance Study of Logically-Modified Heap Sort Algorithm

Bhanu Prakash Lohani[1], Pradeep K. Kushwaha[2], Abhijeet Ashri[3], Mohit Aggarwal[4], Akhil V. Raj[5]

Senior Lecturer, Department of Computer Engineering, AMITY University Gr Noida Campus [1,2]

Scholar, Department of Computer Engineering, AMITY University Gr. Noida Campus [3, 4,5]

ABSTRACT

Today there are several efficient algorithms that cope with the popular task of sorting. This paper presents the comparison between the classical heap sort and the new logical heap sort, which is a start for us. The reason of starting with heap sort was mainly because;it's one of the efficient algorithms in sorting the elements for us, today. Many tests between the classical heap sort and the modified heap sort were run to lead us to the conclusion of this paper. We look forward to discover new logics in algorithms to make them more efficient using Vedic Mathematics. In short, make the algorithm reach its destination much faster.

Keywords: Complexity, Performance of Algorithm, Heapsort, Sorting, Heap Property

INTRODUCTION

A heap is either a large area of memory which is used by the programmer to dynamically allocate or de-allocate them or, it is a balance, left-justified binary tree where every parent's value is larger compared to its children. The heap sort uses the second definition[1].The heap sort, at present, is one of the fastest sorting algorithms with both its worst case and average case runtime being the same, $O(n \log n)$[3]. Thus, it makes the algorithm most important in the sorting category. Heap sort is a comparison-based sorting algorithm. In the classical heap sort, a max or the min heap is formed before the sorting takes place. In the max heap, the largest element present in the whole heap is shifted to the top. Whereas, in the min heap the minimum element present in the heap is shifted to the top of the heap[2]. The minimum element (from the min-heap) or the maximum element (from the max-heap) is extracted from the heap, till none remains in it, the values extracted in a sorted order[3]. Each extraction from the heap puts the element at the last empty location in the array in a sorted order, the rest of it being unsorted. For heap sort to be applied, the tree has to obey the heap property. The property states that every node's children should have smaller value compared to the nodes' value itself[5]. If at any point in the heap we find it being disobeyed, we compare the values from among the node and its children, and then put the larger value in the parent. This process continues till every node in the heap, follows this property.

THE HEAP SORT

How the heap sort works, we have considered the following situation.

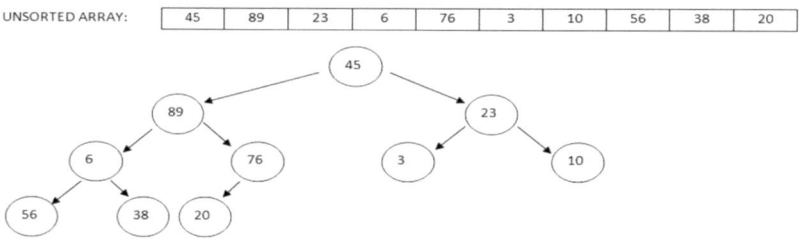

Fig 1.

The unsorted array taken by us, is constructed into somewhat we call a tree structure. Each node of the tree has either two children or, one child or, has no child at all. The ones with no child are called as the Leaf nodes. Each node of a tree consists of three parts- left child, the value of node &, the right child[8]. A node not having either of the children will have the value NULL. Now, each node will occupy 12 bytes- for a 32-bit system, which will make it needing more space on the memory. We surely do not want that as our aim is not only to speed up the process, but also require less space on our system. What we really follow is that instead of constructing the tree itself, we imagine it as a tree and instead of using pointers to point to the left & right of the node, we assign values to it as follows[10],

$$LEFT = 2*I;$$
$$RIGHT = (2*i) + 1;$$

For heap sort to be done, we need each node of the tree to follow the *heap property,* i.e.

$$Value\ (ROOT) > value\ (LEFT);$$
$$Value\ (ROOT) > value\ (RIGHT);$$

The parent in the heap is always the largest when compared to both its children. All leaf nodes will automatically follow the heap property[11]. A tree is a heap if all the nodes in it follow the heap property. If the heap property is found to be violated then, we exchange the value of the largest among the 3 nodes with the root's value.

The first step in heap sorting is to build a MAX_ or MIN_HEAP.

```
void BUILD_MAX_HEAP(int A[])
{
   heapSize = A.length;
    for (int i=heapSize/2; i>=0;i--)
      {
      MAX_HEAPIFY(A, i);
      }
}
```

The creation of max heap or the min heap depends on the requirement of user. If sorting is to be done in ascending order, a max heap is built. Else, a min heap is built. In this function itself, another procedure MAX_HEAPIFY is called.

```
void MAX_HEAPIFY(int A[],int i)
{
  int r,l;
  l=LEFT(i);
  r=RIGHT(i);
  int largestElementIndex=i;
  if((l<heapSize)&&(A[l]>A[i]) )
    {
     largestElementIndex = l;
    }
  else if( (r<heapSize)&&( A[r]>A[largestElementIndex]) )
    {
     largestElementIndex = r;
    }
  if(largestElementIndex!=i)
    {
        int temp = A[i];
        A[i]=A[largestElementIndex];
        A[largestElementIndex]=temp;
       MAX_HEAPIFY(A, largestElementIndex);
    }
}
```

This goes on building the heap by ignoring the leaf nodes (done by taking "i=heapSize/2" in BUILD_MAX_HEAP()), and covers up all the nodes. The step wise iteration of the process is shown by the following snippets:

IN NORMAL HEAP SORT: AFTER STEP 1 - MAX-HEAP:-

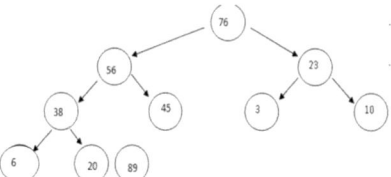

Fig. 2a

AFTER STEP 2 MAX-HEAP:

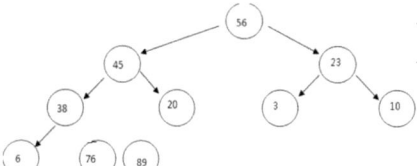

Fig. 2b

AFTER STEP 3 MAX- HEAP :

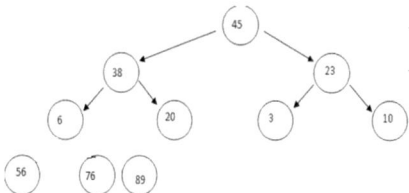

Fig. 2c

The final result of the process is as shown in figure 3.

MAX-HEAP:

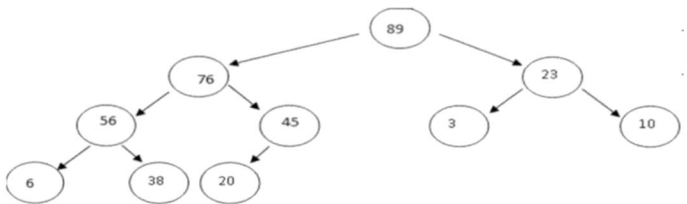

Fig. 3

This is how the working of heap sort is done. The procedure till now is common to our modified algorithm. The algorithm changes from here on.

```
void HEAP_SORT(int A[])
{
  BUILD_MAX_HEAP(A);
  for(int i=A.length-1;i>=1;i--)
  {
    int temp = A[0];
    A[0]=A[i];
    A[i]=temp;
    heapSize = heapSize-1;
    MAX_HEAPIFY(A,0);
  }
}
```

THE LOGICALLY-MODIFIED ALGORITHM

Till now, we had kept exchanging the root element with the last element in the max heap one-by-one.What we tried, was exchanging 2 nodes at the same time which required less number of comparisons with each other and also, required less number of looping.

```
void HEAP_SORT(int A[])
{
  BUILD_MAX_HEAP(A);
  for(int i=A.length-1;i>=1;i-=2)
  {
    int temp = A[0];
    A[0]=A[i];
    A[i]=temp;
    heapSize = heapSize-1;
    if(i>2 && A[1]>A[2])
    {
      temp = A[1];
      A[1]=A[i-1];
      A[i-1]=temp;
      heapSize = heapSize-1;
      MAX_HEAPIFY(A,1);
    }
    else if(i>2)
```

```
{
  temp = A[2];
  A[2]=A[i-1];
  A[i-1]=temp;
  heapSize  = heapSize-1;
  MAX_HEAPIFY(A,2);
}
MAX_HEAPIFY(A,0);
}
}
```

This part of the algorithm is the modified algorithm of ours. The working of our logic is shown in following snippets,

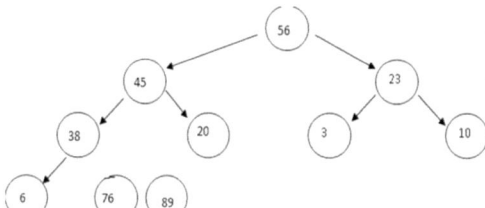

Fig. 4a – Iteration 1

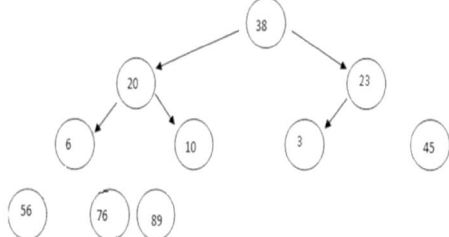

Fig. 4b- Iteration 2

3ᴿᴰ ITEREATION:

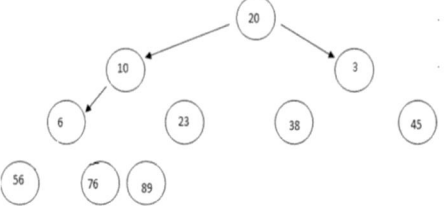

Fig. 4c

4ᵀᴴ ITERATION:

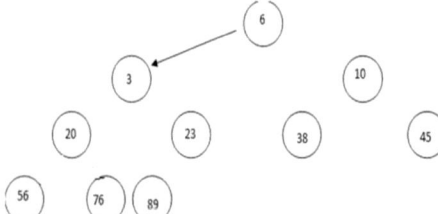

Fig. 4d

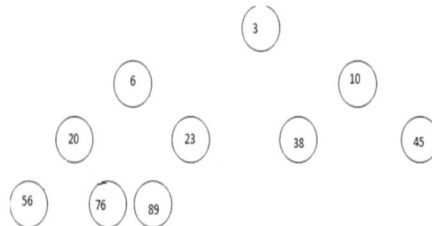

Fig. 4e

FINAL SORTED ARRAY:	3	6	10	20	23	38	45	56	76	89

PERFORMANCE ANALYSIS

The following table gives out the average sorting time of both the heap sort and the modified heap sort algorithm. The values are taken randomly.

Table 1
(Time in nanoseconds)

No. of data items	10	50	100	1000
HeapSort	18965	72859	163110	1087720
Modified HeapSort	16558	69720	155266	876848

CONCLUSION

We have implemented both the algorithms for different number of data items. Our algorithm has successfully worked on limited data we had taken, and got satisfactory results. We have applied our algorithm for different number of data items, and also ran the algorithm in the worst possible case. The results of both algorithms varied and can be seen in the table above.

FUTURE SCOPE

What we are now trying is to seek, in the near future, a way to make our own algorithm more efficient, if possible. We are to do this by taking the help of Vedic Mathematics, which attempts on solving our day-to-day complex problems in the most efficient way.If it's possible anyhow, to implement the same logic in our algorithm, our aim of making the algorithm running much faster, that is, reaching their destination much faster than before, will be fulfilled. Our target is not only heap sort, but some of the many algorithms where our aim of research and analysis can be fulfilled.

REFERENCES

[1] Knuth D.E *The art of programming-sorting andsearching.*2nd edition AddisonWesley.
[2] Hoare C A R Quicksort. Computer journal 5(1):10~15.
[3] I.Wegner:*BOTTOM-UP-HEAPSORT beating on averageQUICKSORT(if n is not very small).* Proceedings of theMFCS90, LNCS 452,516-522, 1990
[4] S.Carlsson: *Avariant of HEAPSORT with almost optimalnumber of comparisons.* Information Processing Letters24:247-250, 1987.
[5] I.Wegner:*The worst case complexity of Mc diarmid andReed's variant of BOTTOM-UP-HEAP SORT is less thannlogn+1.1n.* Proceedings of the STACS91, LNCS 480:137-147, 1991.
[6] Xio dong wang,ying jie wu *an improved heap sortalgorithm with nlogn –0.788928n comparisons in worstcase.* Journal of computer science andtechnology22 (6):898~903
[7] S. Haldar: "Heapsort with $n\ log(n+1) + n - 2log(n+1)-2$ key comparisons using $\lfloor\ n/2\ \rfloor$ additional bits", Technical Report RUU-CS-93-14, April 1993.
[8] PankajSareen, "Comparison of Sorting Algorithms (On Basis of Average Case)", IJARCSSE, Volume-3, Issue-3, March 2013.
[9] Cormen T., Leiserson C., Rivest R., and Stein C., Introduction to Algorithms, McGraw Hill, 2001.
[10] Vandana Sharma, Satwinder Singh and Dr. K. S. Kahlon, "Performance Study of Improved Heap Sort Algorithm and Other Sorting Algorithms on Different Platforms", IJCSNS International Journal of Computer Science and Network Security, VOL.8 No.4, April 2008
[11] Sorting Algorithms. Online.http://people.cs.ubc.ca/~harrison/Java/sorting-demo.html